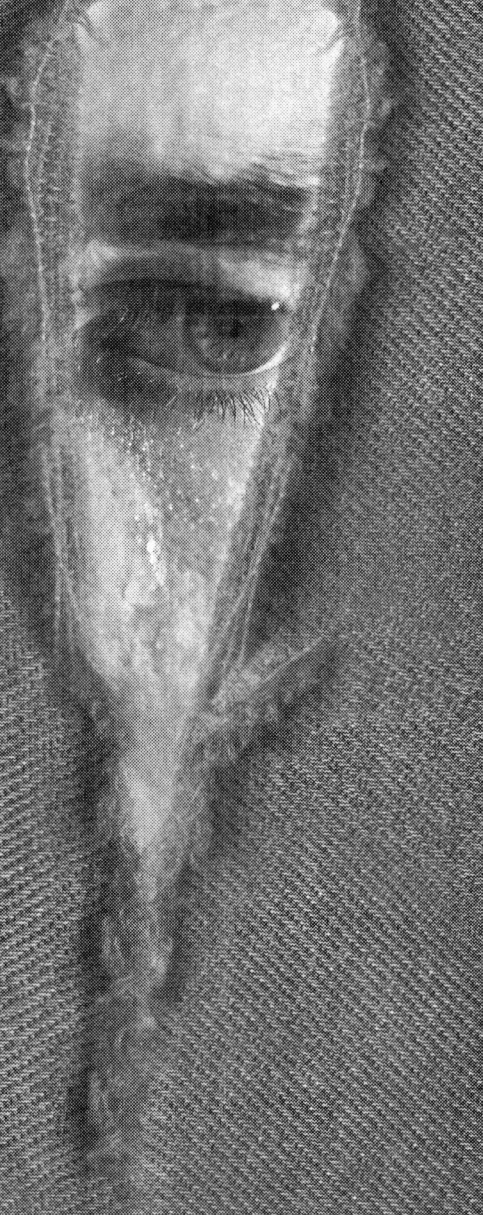

More than a Tear

A Shiva Guide for Mourners and Consolers

Yigal Segal

More Than A Tear

by Yigal Segal

Copyright @ 2013 Yigal Segal

Notice of Rights

All rights reserved. No part of this book may be reproduced or utilized in any form or by any means, electronic or mechanical, including photocopying, recording, or by any information storage and retrieval system, without written permission from the author. Reviewers may quote brief passages.

ISBN 978-0-9888057-0-5 (Hard Copy)
ISBN 978-0-9888057-1-2 (ePub)

Cover Design by Ben Gasner

Page Layout by Staiman Design

Edited and proofing by Chava Willig Levy and Shimon Apisdorf

Distributed to the trade by the Jewish Literacy Foundation:
jliteracy12@gmail.com

Distributed to Judaica stores by Judaica Press:
(800) 972-6201 or (718) 972-6200

Available for purchase on the web at www.guidetoshiva.com

The author encourages feedback, questions, and comments via email at guidetoshiva@gmail.com

This is a marvelously written short book about grieving, comforting and dealing with the eventual mortality that faces us all. It is halachically accurate, psychologically insightful and written clearly and compassionately. I am certain that it will be a source of strength and comfort to many, whether scholar or of the laity.

Rabbi Berel Wein, Director, Destiny Foundation

Yigal Segal has demonstrated the admirable ability to present the Torah's answers to our age old questions about grief and mourning in a clear and practical manner. He masterfully draws upon authentic Torah sources, but transforms them into a language that all can understand. This book carefully avoids technical issues and complicated jargon, and gets right to the point. I recommend this book to all who suffer loss, and all who wish to lend comfort to others who are grieving. I especially recommend it as a manual for Rabbis, counselors, and others who face these issues frequently.

Rabbi Dr. Tzvi Hersh Weinreb
Executive Vice President Emeritus, Orthodox Union

We all make Shiva calls and, inevitably, we will sit Shiva ourselves. Yet, we know so little about this ritual. This lovely volume is a wonderful companion to Shiva, its origins and practices.

Ari L. Goldman, author of "Living a Year of Kaddish."

It was our great merit
to have Rivka and Yigal Segal as
friends, neighbors and teachers
in their time living in Atlanta,
GA. Though much younger than
we were, they taught us through
their actions and their words. It is
an honor to be a sponsor of this
special guide to the laws of Shiva
in their honor.

**May the memory of
Yigal's father and brother
serve as a blessing
to all of K'lal Yisroel.**

Shirley and Perry
Brickman

Like many children of Holocaust survivors, the concept of grandparents was foreign to me. Each of my parents were the sole survivors of their families. Though they never had the opportunity to mourn the profound losses they suffered, they worked hard to pass along the traditions that they remembered from their childhood.

This book is dedicated to the family I was never privileged to meet: to my **grandparents, aunts and uncles** who perished in the Holocaust.

It is also dedicated to the memory of my father, **Harold Singer**, who was able to preserve and pass along the laws and traditions of a people that was targeted for annihilation.

May their memories be preserved

Marc A. Singer

In memory of my husband,
Rabbi Zev Segal zt"l

and my son,
Moshe Yonah Segal zt"l

May their memories
be a blessing
for our entire family.

Esther Segal

Notes and Acknowledgements

Writing this book was one of the most difficult tasks I have ever undertaken. Reviewing the laws and customs of Shiva, and researching grief and mourning, brought back difficult experiences with such force that it felt like I was beginning the mourning process all over again. I have to thank Hashem for giving me the inner strength to complete this project despite its many challenges.

In most of the chapters, I use the masculine "he" or "him" to describe a mourner. This was done to make the flow of the text easier for the reader, but all Shiva laws and customs apply equally to men and women unless specifically indicated in the book.

There are many to acknowledge and thank for their part in making this book a reality.

Dr. Marc Singer is more than a friend. He is like a brother to me and has been with me every step of the way of this process. He was instrumental in conceiving and developing the idea for this book. Marc and I went through our respective Shivas together and took our experiences and invested them in this project. I am deeply grateful for his support and encouragement and I am proud that we achieved our goal of publishing this book. Thanks Doc, for everything.

My personal impetus for writing this book was the recent passing of both my father, Rabbi Zev Segal, z"l and my brother, Moshe Segal, z"l. My mother, Mrs. Esther Segal, who should live until 120 years, has been the epitome of strength in dealing with these two tragedies in her life, and as I have always done, I try to emulate her grace and ability to cope with difficult circumstances. I thank her for everything she has done to bring this book to print and I wish her only continued nachas from her children, grandchildren, and great grandchildren.

Editing a book is a difficult task and I thank Chava Willig Levy for her ability to transform a sentence while keeping the voice of the author intact. My years of work in the Jewish Literacy Foundation with my friend and partner, Shimon Apisdorf, allowed me a bird's eye view of how a real author writes. I thank him for all his help on this project.

Jeremy Staiman did a masterful job of typesetting this book and I thank him for his efforts and his friendship. Ben Gasner's cover design captured the essence of what we wanted to convey and I appreciate the opportunity to benefit from his great talent and expertise. I also want to thank Shloime Ash for suggesting the title of the book.

I also want to thank the following people for their assistance in this project: Baruch Cohen, Rabbi Hillel David, Ari Goldman, Rabbi Ephraim Greenblatt, Rabbi Paysach Krohn, Rabbi Yosef Zvi Rimon, Rabbi Dovid Solomon, Chaim Spero and Rabbi Dr. Tzvi Hersh Weinreb.

I could not have written this without the encouragement of my brother, Nachum Segal. I thank him for everything, especially for being a friend.

We recently lost my wife's grandfather, Phillip Grossman, z"l, who was a major part of our lives. We wish Dorothy "Grandma" Grossman many years of good health and *Yiddishe nachas* from her family in her new home in Jerusalem.

G-d has blessed us with a beautiful family and each one of our children has a special part in helping me with everything I try to accomplish. Chani, Akiva, Yosef, Neemi, Zviki, Yehuda, Yedidya

Zev and Matanya: I love you all very much and thank Hashem for you every day. May you continue to grow and be the best that you can be!

Finally, I want to thank my wife, Rivki. She is a constant inspiration to me and her influence is present on every page of this book. Baruch Hashem, we have merited to live with our family in Jerusalem for the last seven years. May G-d give us the strength and insight to continue to do our part in whatever master plan He has for us.

Yigal Segal
Jerusalem, 2012

Table of Contents

Foreword by Dr. Marc Singer 1

Introduction 5

Chapter 1 – What is Grief? 9

Chapter 2 – The Origins of Shiva 17

Chapter 3 – The Duality of Shiva.. 23

Chapter 4 – The Meaning behind the Laws and
                   Customs of Shiva.. 29

Chapter 5 – The Sounds of Silence 39

Chapter 6 – A Quick Guide 47

Afterword – Shiva Is Over. Now What? 69

Appendix – Kaddish 73

Endnotes 77

Foreword

*A*lthough part of my medical training included accepting the fact that patients die, I still was not prepared for the loss of my first patient. I could hardly expect to be prepared for the loss of my parent.

During my twenty-five plus years of practicing medicine, I have been privileged to care for many patients with a wide range of illnesses. I quickly learned that although the relationships and successes were gratifying, they would always be tempered by losses along the way. Although it never got easier, I realized early on that

I had to accept the inevitable. As I was taught, Rule One was that patients die. Rule Two was that you couldn't do anything about Rule One. To maintain a proper stance at all times, I had to teach myself to remain professional in the face of sadness.

As I built up the barrier between myself and death, I wondered how I would feel when I would suffer a personal loss. After all, death is inevitable. I knew that, one day, I would need to grieve over a loss of my own.

That day came when my father succumbed to a long and painful illness. I now had to experience my own grief and mourning. Like so many others, I knew something of the mechanics of Shiva. I knew that it would give me the framework in which to mourn. But I wondered, would I be able to cry as I felt I should? Would this be another death on the other side of the wall I had constructed? Would no tears come?

When the Torah enumerates the festivals, we are commanded to rejoice in the holidays. I was always struck by how the Torah can command one to be happy. The definitive law book tells us what to do, how to act and interact, but can it command us how to feel? Does the commandment apply if you had a bad day, week or month?

As I went through the stages of mourning, things began to make sense to me. Just as the Torah commands us to be happy and our Rabbis clarify how to be happy, the week of Shiva provides the blueprint needed to express our sadness. This framework is necessary, because until one has buried a relative, until one sits low to the floor, one is never really prepared for how to mourn.

There is a certain club that mourners belong to, a certain bond they share. Having someone to help alleviate the grief is invaluable. Yigal Segal and I live six thousand miles away from each other. And yet, when we each lost our father, we were there for each other, helping each other through Shiva. After we experienced our respective Shiva observances, we realized that no one can be prepared to observe Shiva and to grieve on command. Yes, each person grieves differently. Merely knowing that—and knowing that it is acceptable both to cry AND not to cry—gave us comfort. That's when we came up with the concept of this book, a guide for the inevitable Shiva period that everyone eventually experiences. But we soon realized that mourners weren't the only ones needing guidance. So many of us walk into a Shiva house, wondering anxiously what to say and how to act. And so this guide for both the mourner and the visitor was born.

It is my hope that this guide will find its way into many houses of mourning and that it will serve as a companion, answering both the why and the how of Shiva observance. Yes, the rabbis gave us a framework in which to grieve, just as they helped to define how to rejoice during the festivals. This volume is intended not only to delineate those laws, but to look at the reasons why they exist. Like any guide, it cannot be all-inclusive. However, it is intended to serve as a foundation for the philosophy, customs and laws of Jewish mourning. When someone passes away, the departed leaves a void. Mourning is a journey that helps us cope with that void. This compendium is intended to help us navigate that journey.

We hope mourners and their comforters will find this book useful as both a legal text and a map to the mysteries of mourning. It is intended for families and visitors alike.

After all, the loss is shared by everyone. May we all be comforted.

Marc A. Singer, MD
New York, 2012

Introduction

*S*hiva: The etymology of the word is simple. It is the number seven in Hebrew, representing the number of days one sits in mourning after the death of a close relative. The word is probably one of the most recognizable in the Jewish religion as everyone at one point in their life goes through the experience of "sitting Shiva." However, because of the custom not to discuss the laws and traditions of mourning before we actually have to fulfill them, few people are prepared for Shiva before they experience it.

Our generation is blessed with a profusion of literature about Aveilut, the long-term process of mourning. Still, one need seemed unmet: an easily accessible volume devoted exclusively to the week of Shiva. This guide tries to address two issues: how to pay a proper Shiva visit and how to be prepared for Shiva's customs and obligations until the opportunity to consult a Rabbi presents itself.

A Shiva visit is truly one of Judaism's most difficult-to-master acts of kindness. At first glance you might wonder, "What's the big deal about paying a Shiva call? All I have to do is walk in, sit down for a few minutes and express my condolences." It sounds simple, but even with the best of intentions, you might say something improper or ask inappropriate questions. Out of embarrassment, you might opt for condolence cards or in memoriam donations from then on. Ultimately, that might deprive another mourner of your empathic presence.

You may have read stories recounted in the Talmud of great Rabbis consoling friends with words that may seem beyond comprehension. For example, Rabbi Yochanan would show mourners a small bone, with him at all times, explaining that it was from the tenth son that had predeceased him. Why? So they would know that whatever they were going through couldn't be as bad as what he endured. Can you believe that? He had TEN children die and *he* was comforting others? How did he even get up in the morning? What spiritual and emotional fortitude! Does G-d hold us to the same standard, or was this behavior reserved for saintly people like Rabbi Yochanan?

We find similar, seemingly incomprehensible stories recorded much more recently. The Chofetz Chaim, Rabbi Yisrael Meir Kagan, one of the leading sages of the early 20th century, was visiting Warsaw when his son Avraham passed away in his hometown of Radin. After receiving a telegram to return home immediately, the Chofetz Chaim arrived just as his son's funeral ended. Without tears or any other manifestation of grief, he declared, "G-d has given, G-d has taken. May G-d's name be blessed forever." He then spoke of a Jewish mother who, during the Spanish Inquisition, watched her two sons die before her eyes. She looked up to heaven and said, "Master of the World, I admit that when my sons were alive, my love for You was incomplete. After all, part of my heart also loved them. Now that my children have died, all my love is dedicated to You. Only now can I fulfill the commandment, 'And you shall love Hashem, your G-d, with all your heart, with all your soul, and with all your might.'" The Chofetz Chaim then cried out, "Master of the World, all the love I felt for my son, I now dedicate to You!"[1]

I read this story and sat in my chair, stunned. How could any human being make these declarations after suffering such a terrible tragedy? Is this reaction expected of all mourners, no matter what loss they endured? Do we have an obligation to console a mourner with the Chofetz Chaim's words?

Stories like these accentuate the guidance we all need—mourners and comforters alike. No two people react identically to a loved one's death, even if mourning the same loved one! I have sat Shiva twice in the last five years, each time under very different circumstances.

My father's tragic disappearance and death prompted a spectacular outpouring of Shiva visits and condolence calls. My brother's death from esophageal cancer, a harrowing nine-month odyssey, was a more private but no less tragic loss. Both Shiva experiences left me with a lot of questions and a burning quest to find answers. This book charts that quest.

I have not researched every available source—Biblical, Talmudic or otherwise—and I claim no more expertise than anyone else. Rather, I have tried to gather a cross-section of religious and secular sources addressing death and bereavement. The result, this anthology, explores ways to make mourning and comforting more meaningful for everyone. As for the Jewish perspective, I have tried to compile a practical guide to Shiva's laws and customs, offering their sources whenever possible. I hope this will enable both mourner and comforter to have a more meaningful Shiva experience.

"*He will eliminate death forever, and G-d will erase tears from all faces...*"

(Isaiah 25:8)

1

What is Grief?

*B*efore we explore the origin of Shiva, we need to clarify what happens to a mourner after the death and burial of a loved one. When we lose someone close to us, we enter a world of grief and mourning. Let's define these two terms. Webster's Dictionary defines grief as "intense emotional suffering caused by loss, disaster, misfortune, etc.; acute sorrow; deep sadness." Mourning is defined as "the actions or feelings of someone who mourns; specifically, the expression of grief at someone's death." Mourning is more closely associated with death. Grief, in contrast, can be a response to many different losses, such as the loss of one's job or a decline in one's health. We tend to separate the grief over a loved one's death from these other circumstances but, in essence, they all represent a form of loss.[2]

Grief is a painful process which Dr. Elisabeth Kübler-Ross, author of the classic *On Death and Dying*, divided into five stages: Denial, Anger, Bargaining, Depression, and Acceptance.[3] Hundreds of books have been written about these stages, among the most accepted approaches to grief. An essential point in Kübler-Ross's theory is that no two people experience these five stages in precisely the same way. For some, denial can take minutes; for others, decades. The fact that grieving has no fixed timetable can be very frustrating for those surrounding the mourner.

Jewish tradition dictates that the official mourning period following a parent's death is one year (or, more precisely, twelve lunar months). In contrast, the official mourning period following the death of a sibling, child or spouse is one lunar month. In part, this contrast reminds us that grieving is a process. Each person experiences that process differently. For some, any loss elicits the same response; for others, the loss of a particular relative triggers a particular response. Some mourners heal quickly; others are sure their grief will never end.

A friend of mine had a sister, with whom he was not particularly close, who unfortunately was diagnosed with terminal cancer. During the eight months of her illness, and after her death, he was in a deep depression, unable to cope with his loss. His wife just couldn't understand his intense grief. "It's very sad that she got sick and passed away," she would tell him, "but you weren't close to her when she was alive. Why are you still grieving for her?" From his wife's perspective, it was over and done with; from his, he was in the middle of a process with no end in sight.

I recently came across a book entitled When There Are No Words by Charlie Walton. The loss Charlie and his family endured was horrific. Two of his sons, along with their close friend, died from carbon monoxide poisoning while sitting in their car. Charlie writes about the 3:25 AM knock at the door. He paints a vivid picture of the hours following the accident. He speaks of trying to make himself cry. Like many others, Charlie was able to cry on happy occasions or maybe even during a tearjerker movie, but now, after the greatest calamity anyone could imagine, he just couldn't cry. Guilt stricken, he tried to shed tears, but they just wouldn't come. He eventually learned a lesson from this, a lesson we all need to learn: *Your natural response to grief is the right response for you*[4]. It doesn't matter what you or others expect. It doesn't matter what conventional wisdom dictates. The way you grieve is the way *you* need to grieve.

One psychologist writes that grief counseling is a waste of time and money. Since everyone has their own unique way of grieving, it is impossible for a counselor to pinpoint the specifics of that person's grief, let alone recommend how to cope with it. This insight is crucial if we are to understand a mourner's mindset. Everyone grieves differently, no matter what circumstances cause the grief.

Rabbi Maurice Lamm is renowned for his groundbreaking book, *The Jewish Way in Death and Mourning* (Jonathan David Publishers, 1969), a must for any Jew mourning for a loved one. Soon after my father passed away, I was surprised to learn from a close friend that Rabbi Lamm had written a second book on the subject: *Consolation* (Jewish Publication Society, 2005). In this masterful work, Rabbi Lamm explores a myriad of issues connected to grief and mourning. He writes about the *process* of mourning, how we deal with the death of a close relative as time goes by. At one point, he describes what happens to a mourner before reaching grief's fifth and final stage: acceptance. He explains that before we are able to redefine our relationship with the deceased, *"we experience an uncommon confusion—not necessarily delirium or chaos or even bewilderment but rather dislocation, a form of discontinuity. We sense that something is out of sync, but we cannot quite decode it.....During our loved one's lifetime, we were safe within a circumference of images and memories—the departed and the family and our friends—and now this world is simply not the same. We are disoriented."*[5]

Disorientation is what grief is all about. We are evicted from our normal routine, our normal lives. The person for whom we grieve was part of a stable picture in a frame that included us, and now that frame is broken. The picture is torn, and we struggle to deal with the new reality.

So what about the Chofetz Chaim and Rabbi Yochanan, mentioned in this book's introduction? Did they experience the five stages? Did they go through disorientation? I can't answer those questions because everyone grieves differently, and these Torah giants are not necessarily being held up as ideals for us to measure ourselves against. These two men had such firm faith in the Almighty, such a close connection to Him, that their reaction to tragedy surely differed from ours. Maybe their behavior is what we need to emulate, but not necessarily duplicate. Maybe our Sages shared the story about Rabbi Yochanan to teach us that his behavior was not strange, and no matter how we react to the death of our loved one, neither is ours.

In the Tractate of Eruvin (46a), Shmuel teaches us that when it comes to mourning practices, the law is to follow the lenient opinion. It seems strange: Why would Shmuel use the term "halacha," or law, to say we should be lenient? Couldn't he simply say that when it comes to mourning, you can be lenient if you want to be? Is it our *obligation* to be lenient? Shmuel understood that people may experience countless reactions when a loved one dies. He wanted us to know that the law is to do what you feel you need to do, to cope with your loss *your way*, within the framework of Shiva's process, laws and customs. If you feel you need to be stringent to cope with your loss, so be it, but you are obligated to find your own path to achieving comfort. (Rabbi Lamm expresses a similar idea in *Consolation*.[6])

Jewish law's insightful approach to different types of grief is illustrated by these all-too-real questions: Must one mourn for adoptive parents? What about stepparents? And what about biological parents who were abusive? Rabbi Dr. Joel Wolowelsky deals with all these questions in two separate articles.[7] Although biological parents bring a child into the world, the importance of those who raise that child is undeniable. However, certain halachic consequences arise when mourning an adoptive parent.

Quoting Rabbi Joseph B. Soloveitchik, Dr. Wolowelsky states that one who mourns for an adoptive parent or a stepparent definitely fulfills a mitzvah. The source for this ruling is the Shulchan Aruch,[8] (the Code of Jewish Law) which states that if someone died and left behind no mourners, ten worthy men should assemble in his home for all seven days of mourning, and others should come and comfort them. Rav Soloveitchik would advise mourners to sit Shiva for their adoptive parent based on this ruling, which establishes that one fulfills the mitzvah of mourning even when there is no halachic obligation to mourn.

Dr. Wolowelsky analyzes mourning an abusive parent by considering whether one is halachically obliged to mourn an evil person. He refers to a concept that is also mentioned by Dr. Therese Rando in her book about grieving[9]: Mourning relatives with whom you had a painful or conflicted relationship allows you to grieve for the love you couldn't share with them when they were alive. Wolowelsky theorizes that "opting out of the mourning process would only cement the lifelong feeling of betrayal….. [Mourning an abusive parent] might just inspire individuals to seek help in coming to peace with their past."[10] The healing embedded in the Shiva experience can allow these mourners to look forward while coming to grips with their past. Nevertheless, the halacha exempts abused children from sitting Shiva if they would suffer emotional distress because of it.

Rav Soloveitchik seems to have taken into account the mourner's psychological state when he rendered his decisions about adoptive children, stepchildren and abused children. Recognizing that grief has many subjective faces, he allowed adopted children and stepchildren to experience the unique healing that sitting Shiva can provide. However, recognizing that abused children might be grieving as well but in a very different way, he gave them the option not to sit Shiva if it intensified their distress. Wolowelsky shows us again that grief manifests itself in countless ways. Demonstrating their sensitivity to this reality, our Rabbis have tailored mourning in general—and Shiva in particular—to meet each mourner's individual needs.

2

The Origins of Shiva

*I*n the previous chapter, we explored how the Shiva period and its customs are designed to help each mourner deal in his or her own way with a loved one's death. We now turn to the questions: What are the origins of Shiva? How did it come about?

The Torah's first mention of a seven-day mourning period occurs after the death of our forefather, Jacob.[11] Joseph and his brothers bring his body to the land of Israel for burial, and right before this is completed, we read, *"And they made a mourning period of seven days."*[12] What's fascinating is that an extended period of time had already gone by since Jacob's passing. We know this because the Torah mentions a forty-day embalming period observed while Jacob's sons were still in Egypt. Nevertheless, Joseph established an additional week of mourning in the land of Israel. Also, according to the Torah's sequence of events, this week seems to have occurred before Jacob's final burial, unlike the Shiva of today, which cannot begin until after burial.[13]

Possibly because of this, the Rabbis of the Talmud mention another source for Shiva, derived from a verse in Amos (8:10): "*And I will turn your festivals (Chageichem) into days of mourning.*" From this, the Talmud teaches that just as the holiday of Sukkot (referred to in the Torah as Chag) lasts for seven days, the initial period of mourning also lasts for seven days. This comparison leaves us with a serious question: Why would the Rabbis compare a joyous holiday to our classic mourning period? Just because a period of intense happiness lasts for seven days, a period of mourning and despair has the same length of time assigned to it? What possible connection can there be between such vastly different events?

But that's not the only paradox. The mourning process has much in common with Jewish wedding celebrations! For example, it is customary at Jerusalem funerals to make seven circuits around the grave, just as a bride circles her groom seven times under the chuppah (wedding canopy). Also, the Talmud (Moed Katan 28b) teaches us that the mourner sits at the head of the room, and so does the bridegroom. Furthermore, the Talmud (Ketuvot 8a-

b) mentions that the blessing for a groom and the blessing for a mourner[14] both require a quorum of ten.

How can two of life's most contradictory events have so much in common? How can the intense sadness of losing a loved one compare to the joy of starting a new life with one's spouse?

To solve this mystery, we need to examine these events' one common denominator: seven days.

The number seven has many applications in Jewish life. Let's take a moment to examine this number and see how it sheds light on our dilemma.

The Torah mentions the number seven for the first time at the beginning. We are used to saying that G-d created the world in six days and "rested" on the seventh but, in actuality, the seven days of Creation are a complete unit in which Shabbat is an integral part. The spark of our entire existence was created in the space of seven days.

The number seven plays other important roles in Jewish life: The laws of Shmittah require us to let the land of Israel lie fallow every seven years. One who has become impure through interaction with a dead body must follow a seven-day process to regain spiritual purity. The counting of the Omer takes seven weeks, corresponding to the time it took our nation to journey from Egypt to Mount Sinai, where G-d gave us the Torah. That the number seven is significant is obvious, but what does it really mean?

The number seven represents the time needed to reach a new reality. Seven days pass and we have a new world; seven years, and there is a new land of Israel waiting to be replanted; seven days, and we have regained spiritual purity; seven weeks, and we are now ready to become a new nation, committed to G-d's Torah.

Seven is not only the number of transition, it is the number of transformation. Realizing this, our greatest leader, Moshe Rabbeinu (Moses), established seven days for two of life's biggest transformations: gaining a loved one and losing a loved one.[15]

This helps us understand why our Sages ordained that the Shiva process begin after burial takes place.[16] To move into a new phase of life, closure is necessary. We have to say goodbye to what used to be, or else the Shiva process won't work as it should. Burial is the final step, totally removing any physical connection to the person we have lost. Once the body is buried, we are forced to see ourselves in this new light: as people missing something, someone precious. Until our loved one has been buried, the needed closure and transition are unattainable.

When Jacob's sons told him that Joseph, his favorite child, was presumed dead, the Torah tells us that *"he refused to be comforted."*[17] Was it because he didn't actually have a body to bury (the only "evidence" his sons presented was Joseph's blood-drenched coat)? Was it because deep down, Jacob believed that Joseph was still alive? We don't know. What we do know is that Jacob had no closure. Because of that, he could not be comforted.

In 2000, my wife and I attended a dinner benefitting an Israeli yeshiva. One of the speakers was a man whose son, missing in action since the first Lebanon War in 1982, had attended the yeshiva. As we listened with a heavy heart, we realized that this man had never been able to let go of his son. He had never been able to move to a new reality because although eighteen years had passed, he still didn't know if his son was actually dead. The pain in this father's eyes and voice left an indelible impression on us as we prayed together with him for some sort of closure, whatever it might be.

You can't move on until you have marked the end of your loved one's life in some way, and that is why Shiva cannot begin until that loved one has been buried. It is a gift of G-d to be able to overcome our grief and pain, and it is only with closure that this process can begin.

Beyond the number seven's significance for coping with our changed lives, having a time limit placed on the grieving process has other benefits. Rabbi Lamm emphasizes this when explaining why our Sages established two distinct mourning limits: twelve lunar months for parents and thirty days for other relatives. *"A person should not commemorate or remember the trauma of death for more than a given amount of time…so as not to strain the mourner's mind to retain an active memory of that death. We could not progress, even survive, if such memories hung around in our acute awareness. They would paralyze us, freeze all of life into one hour, and we could not then make the transition back to living—surely not transcend the death or become transformed and re-energized."*[18] Rabbi Lamm adds that our Sages established annual days of remembrance for deceased relatives (Yartzeit) specifically to counteract G-d's gift of closure so that we will never totally forget our loved ones.

Shiva is the first step toward making peace with the tragedy of losing a relative. Moshe and our Rabbis are sending us a message: You have entered a new reality and we know you need time to cope with that. These first seven days will help you. They will introduce you to that new reality and to the process of coping with all you will experience in the weeks and months to come.

3

The Duality of Shiva

*M*any commentators discuss the dual nature of Shiva: its benefit to both the deceased and the mourner.[19] We know that visiting mourners, just being there for them, can make a huge difference. But how does Shiva benefit the deceased?

Rabbi Yerucham Levovitz, one of the 20th Century's greatest sages, discusses the purpose of mourning the deceased. Quoting his teacher, Rabbi Simcha Zisel of Kelm, he links it to the concept of nosai b'ol im chaveiro: carrying a burden with one's friend.[20] R' Simcha Zisel explains elsewhere[21] that carrying (or sharing) the burden transcends merely "loving your neighbor as yourself" because it requires action. Don't just feel for people or try to understand what they are going through. Rather, do something to help them.

Rabbi Paysach Krohn illustrates this precept with a beautiful story[22]: The principal of a Brooklyn boys' school heard about a little girl who, along with her classmates, had received her first siddur (prayer book) that morning. To celebrate, every student had been asked to bring sweets to share with her classmates. Unfortunately, this child was unable to do so. The principal imagined how she would always associate sadness with what should have been a day of joy. Most of us would have stopped at just feeling bad for the little girl. This man took action. He got the child's phone number and called her that night. He told her that of all the first-grade girls in Brooklyn, she had been chosen to receive a special siddur with her name engraved on the cover. The next morning, he purchased the siddur and mailed it to her. In short, he gave this child a gift she would cherish for the rest of her life. That is what is called carrying the burden: not just empathizing, but actually taking the time and making the effort to ease another's pain.

Our Rabbis teach us that when someone sits Shiva or does any other act required of a mourner, he is carrying some of the deceased's burden. The mourner actually influences his loved one's soul! When done properly, those acts can literally ease the burden that the deceased must now shoulder in the next world.

What is this burden that the soul carries in the next world? Let's take a look at what happens to someone when they die. Whatever information we can glean from our Rabbinic sources can help us understand how to help our loved one's soul during Shiva and beyond.

In what is known as the definitive work on the laws of mourning, the Gesher Hachaim, Rabbi Yechiel Michel Tucazinsky, zt"l, describes the soul's connection to this world after death.[23] He also delineates the parallels between the soul's complex journey in the next world and the mourner's experiences in this world. When a person dies, when his journey begins, his soul is drawn to G-d, just as metal is drawn to a magnet. Simultaneously, the mourner experiences bereavement's first stage, known as Aninut, which lasts from the time of death until burial.[24] Rabbi Tucazinsky describes the first three days after burial as a time when the soul hovers over the body it has just abandoned. This is why the first three days of Shiva have its own set of obligations.[25] He quotes from the Zohar that "*during Shiva, the soul is in a state of confusion. It is travelling back and forth from its house to its grave and from the grave to its house and mourns for its body. After seven days, the soul travels up to a different level of the heavens...*"[26] Accordingly, a mourner sits for seven days and only then continues to the next stage of mourning.

The message is clear: By fulfilling the laws and customs of Shiva, the mourner and his loved one have not lost each other. By fulfilling the laws and customs of Shiva, the mourner is helping his loved one's soul.

Another parallel emerges when the days of Shiva have ended. After enduring the pain and confusion of separating from its body, the soul stands in judgment before G-d. Every deed, both good and bad, is examined. Only then does the soul receive its final reward and punishment. Like the pre- and post-burial events described above, this entire process occurs in stages. Only after twelve months is the final stage completed.[27] The mourner can help the soul immeasurably throughout this painful process. When he grieves for his loved one, genuinely trying to feel the soul's pain and share its burden, G-d's attribute of judgment is diminished. It's as if Divine justice has been served, at least partially, through the mourner's empathy.

We see the same idea in the story of Pinchas, who zealously and publicly killed Zimri in retribution for his shameless and public immorality. G-d said that Pinchas *"turned back my anger from upon the children of Israel when he zealously avenged My vengeance among them, so I did not consume the children of Israel in My vengeance."*[28] G-d had already started punishing us for tolerating this terrible act, and His plague was spreading. While everyone else just stood by Pinchas took action. He couldn't prevent G-d's punishment, but he removed its severity by shouldering what should have been everyone's burden.

Here is what a mourner must consider during (and after) Shiva: We cannot know exactly what the soul is going through, but we do know it will experience painful stages of separation and judgment. By observing the laws and customs of mourning as best we can, and by keeping our loved ones in our thoughts, we can help them get through their ordeal. We might not understand every what, how or why of the Shiva experience. Occasionally, we may feel ignorant or confused or frustrated. Especially then, it helps to focus on this truth: The Shiva experience is helping our loved one's soul.

What role do comforters play in this process? Is their focus only on the mourner, or do they help the deceased as well?

In 1978, Rabbi Ephraim Greenblatt of Memphis, Tennessee, a renowned expert in Jewish law, wrote a letter to Rabbi Dovid Rosenberg of Brooklyn. In it, he asked if one can fulfill the mitzvah of comforting a mourner via telephone, instead of in person. Rabbi Rosenberg replied that one cannot fulfill the mitzvah via telephone because a Shiva visit has two objectives: to comfort the mourner and to comfort the departed one's soul. He reasoned that a phone call only fulfills the first objective. In contrast, comforting the departed one can only occur at the Shiva house.[29] Rabbi Greenblatt disagreed with this answer, as we see from a letter he wrote in 1979 to Rabbi Moshe Feinstein, the Torah giant of that generation. Rabbi Feinstein agreed that it is better to fulfill part of a mitzvah than none at all.[30]

This exchange shows that when paying a Shiva call, we console the mourner *and* the departed one. This has powerful repercussions. Few of us would think that phoning a mourner has halachic ramifications. Of course, we should not hesitate to make that phone call if we can't pay a Shiva visit in person.

Maimonides comments that if you must choose between comforting a mourner and visiting a sick person, the Shiva visit takes precedence because it enables you to help both the living and the dead, not just one living person.[31] Chasidim and Sephardim offer food and drink at the Shiva house so that, by reciting a Bracha (blessing), and giving listeners a chance to respond "Amen", visitors can help purify the departed one's soul and facilitate its rise heavenward.[32] What may seem insignificant to us can have a huge impact in the world above.

In the next chapter, we will explore specific laws and customs of Shiva. As we learn about their importance, we must keep in mind that both mourner and comforter can help the soul shoulder its burden, diminishing its suffering in the next world.

4

The Meaning Behind the Laws and Customs of Shiva

*M*any laws and customs surround the Shiva experience, and understanding their purpose and their origins is essential. That is this chapter's main objective. In addition, we will explore why certain customs mentioned in Halachic sources are no longer observed in today's Shiva homes.

At the end of the 13th Century, Rabbi Shlomo ben Aderet (Rashba) established this rule regarding mourning customs: "If you do not have a firm Halacha in hand, look at how the public acts, and do accordingly."[33] When we're unsure how to act in a Shiva home, tradition is vital. Sometimes we haven't witnessed the customs our parents kept when they sat Shiva. Then, as the Rashba indicated, our community becomes our teacher. Within that halachic framework, we certainly can shape our mourning experience in general and our Shiva experience in particular.[34] Still, exploring common Shiva customs' roots becomes especially important when our family's mourning traditions are not fully known.

The Talmud and other classic texts mention restrictions that we no longer practice. Whatever the reason, the idea is not to jump at every opportunity to make the mourner follow "the letter of the law." In every generation, Torah society may determine that certain mourning practices are not essential.

To illustrate, a mourner no longer overturns his bed, sleeping on its hard wooden slats, let alone every bed he owns! The Shulchan Aruch explains that since non-Jews might call this a form of witchcraft, and because contemporary and ancient beds differ dramatically, this custom is no longer practiced.[35] Another suspended custom is the "Blessing of the Aveilim." Praising G-d despite their grief, mourners recited it when, after burying their loved one, they reached the city streets. The Ramban records a version of the blessing,[36] but his wording suggests that this custom had already been suspended. During Shiva, some Sephardim add a Bracha to Birkat Hamazon (Grace after Meals) that originated in this public blessing.

In contrast, some customs are long-standing. During Shiva, we generally do not remove anything from the house of mourning (this practice evolved from the Halacha that during Shiva, you may not retrieve clothing you lent someone before he became a mourner).[37] A Rabbi we know explained why: In Jewish villages of long ago, only the Rabbi had an extensive Judaica library. When he sat Shiva, people would borrow his books to research something and would never return them!

Because people are rarely prepared for mourning, this chapter will review the sources and significance of common Shiva practices. We hope this will enable mourners to maximize the Shiva experience, giving them and the deceased true comfort. (If you are looking for a short, concise guide to all Shiva laws and customs, please see Chapter 6.)

- Seudat Havra'ah (The Mourner's Meal of Condolence, or Recovery): the first meal mourners eat after burying their loved one. The mourner is not allowed to eat his own food at the first meal of the first day of mourning.[38] This is derived from a sentence in Yechezkel (24:15-18) where G-d tells Yechezkel that although his wife will die in a plague, He doesn't want him to mourn her. G-d adds, *"And the bread of men you should not eat."* Since G-d is directing Yechezkel not to eat the bread of others, the Rabbis infer that other mourners should eat others' food, not their own. Therefore, friends or relatives should feed the mourner, and their meal must include bread.

Rabbeinu Yerucham, a prominent Rabbi of the late 13th century,[39] explains that after a loved one's funeral, a mourner might be too grief-stricken to eat, so G-d obliged others to feed him. The prevailing custom is to serve the bread with hard boiled eggs[40] because they have no opening, just as a mourner initially has no mouth, or words, to express his grief.

- Not wearing leather shoes: Some say mourners do not remove their leather shoes until they reach the Shiva house, but the prevailing custom is to remove them immediately after the burial.[41] The Bais Yosef[42] derives this practice from Yechezkel (24:17), whom G-d commanded, *"..and you shall put your shoe on your foot."* This implies that other mourners do *not* wear shoes. According to most opinions, this prohibition only applies to leather shoes.

- Covering mirrors in the Shiva house: The classic Halachic reason for this custom is that prayer services take place in a Shiva house, and praying in front of a mirror is forbidden.[43] However, Rabbi Maurice Lamm offers an additional reason, linked to every mourner's deep-seated fear: Will I be the next to die? Will my eventual death matter to more than a handful of people? *"The mirror responds to this fear...The* mirror seems magical. Somehow it assures us that we are alive. This is why when someone speaks to you when you are standing in front of a mirror, he or she is often not looking at you but at it. The mirror's drawing power is magnetic; we simply must look into it. It confirms our presence; our life...When we cover the mirror, we mourners no longer find a reflection...When the mirror is covered and we perceive no image reflected, it is an affirmation of our vanishing.

But why does Shiva not allay the fears of mourners by allowing us to keep our mirrors uncovered? The answer is that Shiva, in all its customs, focuses on confronting, not accommodating, our inner thoughts. It prescribes: Remember, don't forget, face the dangers, don't cover them up; express your anger, don't swallow it...Shiva is not a time for alleviating sorrow but for meeting it head on."[44] The covering of the mirror symbolizes our confrontation with death, our need to face our grief right away, which ultimately can bring a greater level of comfort.

- Sitting on or near the floor: We derive this custom from the book of Job (2:13): *"And they sat with him on the ground."* Once again, Rabbi Lamm offers an insight, this time by considering the popular phrase, "sitting Shiva." Sitting, by design, "*is the metaphor of Jewish mourning because it implies thinking, meditating, and contemplating.... Sitting anchors the heart, keeping the griever from losing the sanctity of mourning in a whirlwind of activity...In addition, the active postures.. signify that a person has control of a situation. ..The appropriate posture for grieving is sitting, precisely because it denotes not being in control....We know deep in our hearts that the deceased was not in control, else there would have been no death, and that we are also not in control....the ultimate control is not with human beings but with G-d.*"[45] "*Mourners traditionally sit lower to the ground to be physically closer to the jaws of the earth that have swallowed up the one being mourned.*"[46]

- Working: Generally, conducting business during Shiva - either directly or indirectly - is forbidden. Since the focus should be on the deceased and mourning them, "business as usual" is simply impossible. However, when refraining from work might cause great financial loss, the mourner may delegate tasks during the first three days of Shiva. After that, he may handle them himself, preferably without leaving the Shiva house. However, if the mourner has a business partner, a Rabbi should determine how business should be conducted during Shiva.

- Bathing, Using Oils, Creams or Makeup: These activities are forbidden. However, after consulting a Rabbi, a person with particular sensitivities might be allowed to bathe with certain restrictions.

  The source for this prohibition is Samuel II (14:2). Yoav, King David's general, asks a wise woman from Tekoa to pretend to be a mourner: "*Please wear clothes of a mourner, and do not anoint yourself with oil…*"[47]

- Washing or wearing new (clean) clothing: This prohibition - for the first 30 days of mourning (Shloshim), according to Ashkenazic custom - also derives from Samuel II (14:2). Yoav asks the woman to wear *"clothes of a mourner,"* implying that these clothes were not as nice as new, or clean, clothes.[48]

- Shaving or cutting hair/nails: These prohibitions (even during the Shloshim period)[49] have a biblical origin: Immediately after the high priest Aaron's two sons died while serving in the Tabernacle, G-d warned him and his remaining sons, *"Do not leave your heads unshorn and do not tear your clothes so you will not die; your brothers, the House of Israel, will mourn the inferno that G-d caused,"*[50] which teaches us that although mourning priests were obligated to cut their hair, all other mourners were forbidden to do so.[51]

The topics of Bathing, Clothing, and Shaving are all related to the rejuvenation of one's body and appearance. Unless absolutely necessary, a mourner should not engage in any form of rejuvenation.[52] When our loved one's soul leaves its body and strives for a more spiritual existence, we must share its burden. Ignoring our appearance during Shiva (and Shloshim) is a symbolic departure from the physical world. This not only connects us to our loved one's soul, it allows us to express our personal loss as well.

- Greeting visitors: A mourner should not greet anyone

during Shiva, especially with the word "Shalom," one of G-d's names. Opinions differ about saying "Good Morning" or offering a handshake to a mourner,[53] but our Rabbis share this belief: During this week of mourning, the normal "How are you?" is inappropriate, detracting from a Shiva home's spirituality.

≈ Saying Kaddish (the Mourner's Prayer): This is the most famous Jewish mourning practice. And yet, Kaddish includes not a single word about death! (For a full Hebrew, English and transliterated text of Kaddish, turn to the Appendix) Instead, it focuses on praising G-d. The age-old question is: Why do we recite this of all prayers when we are in mourning?

There is a fascinating thought on the verse, *"Difficult in the eyes of G-d is the death of His devout ones."*[54] These deaths are difficult in G-d's eyes because every person in this world has a unique part of G-d in him. Every person's soul has the task of bringing G-d's glory to our world. When someone dies, that part of G-d has left the world, and G-d Himself feels that something is missing. Kaddish fills that void. When we recite its words in our loved one's memory, we increase G-d's presence in His world. Miraculously, our Kaddish also replenishes what His world lost when our loved one's soul left it.[55] This is just one link between Kaddish and mourning.

The earliest source for Kaddish is a story about the saintly Rabbi Akiva.[56] While visiting a cemetery, he notices a man whose face is blackened and who is carrying a load of thorns. Taking pity on him, Rabbi Akiva asks if perhaps he is a mistreated slave and offers to redeem him. He asks if perhaps the man needs money and offers to help him financially. The man replies that he is dead, punished for having been a tax collector who abused the poor and flattered the rich. Rabbi Akiva asks if there is any way to atone for his sins. The man replies that if a son of his would declare in a synagogue that all should bless G-d's name, and if those present would answer, "May His great Name be blessed forever," his sins would be absolved.

Rabbi Akiva learns that the man's wife had been pregnant when he died. After much searching, he finds the child, a son, and teaches him Torah. The boy enters a synagogue and declares that all should bless G-d's name. When the worshipers reply, "May His great Name be blessed forever," his father's soul is released from its terrible punishment.[57]

Today, nearly 2000 years after Rabbi Akiva's lifetime, the words "May His great Name be blessed forever" remain the centerpiece of the Kaddish prayer.

When we lose a loved one, we search for ways to benefit his soul. As was discussed in Chapter 3, we need to feel and ease its burden. Reciting Kaddish is an essential way to do this. The story of Rabbi Akiva illustrates the power of Kaddish, especially when recited by one's child. Even if we don't see how our actions help our loved one's soul, we know that reciting Kaddish (as well as performing other good deeds) can make a huge difference in the next world.

Kaddish benefits the deceased, but it doesn't have to end there. In *Living a Year of Kaddish*, Ari Goldman asserts that Kaddish is just as much for the living as for the dead. He writes, *"I believe that in my daily recitation of the prayer, I was coming to terms with who my father was and who I am.... When I die, I want my children to say Kaddish for me, but for themselves, too."*[58]

Despite the tragedies we experience, we are obligated to praise G-d, to acknowledge our belief in Him. As we serve Him in this way, we serve the loved one we have lost. But the duality of the mourning experience proves that this simple prayer can aid and comfort the mourner as well.

5

The Sounds of Silence

*F*or many people, visiting a Shiva home is one of the hardest things to do. We are afraid that we won't know what to say or, even worse, that our words will hurt - not comfort - the mourner. People have told me that this book's most important chapter should list what NOT to say at a Shiva house! There are too many horror stories about outrageous things well-meaning visitors have said. I hope this chapter will help in some way, because here is where we will speak about silence.

The Rabbis teach that we need to remain silent in a Shiva house until the mourner addresses us. Why? Aren't we supposed to comfort the mourner? How can we do that by saying nothing?

The Talmud in Brachot (6b) quotes Rav Pappa, who says the reward for visiting a Shiva house is primarily earned through silence. His source is the book of Job (2:13): *"And they sat with him for seven days and seven nights. None spoke a word to him for they saw his pain was very great."* When Job's friends heard what terrible things had happened to him, they sat with him for seven days and seven nights without uttering a single word. NOT ONE WORD! How is that possible? What did they think they were accomplishing by just sitting there?

Their accomplishment's underlying secret was not what they didn't do. It's what they *did* do: They sat *with* Job. They empathized with him. Since there was no way to comfort him with words, they comforted him with silence.

Job's friends taught our Rabbis the key to true comfort: making mourners feel - not hear - that we are with them. We don't try to understand their grief; we try to help them understand it in their own way. We want to give mourners the help **they** need, not the help **we** think they need. Silence enables us to do this. Silence enables us to tell our friend, "We are with you in your time of need. And what you need from us, we will give you. We are here to hear - and help - you." Job was so distraught that he couldn't verbalize his grief. His friends were wise enough to give him time to deal with grief in his own way. They sat with him without imposing their emotions, opinions or insights. They simply were with him.

So often we think we need to come up with some magic words of comfort. And yes, silence intensifies the pressure to say just the right thing that will make the mourner smile and forget his grief. Sometimes those magic words actually make the mourner feel worse, simply because that pressure to "say the right thing" totally backfires. Our Rabbis teach us that this "word search" is ill-advised. In their wisdom, they teach us that silence enables us to hear what the mourner needs. When he or she is ready to tell us, we'll know why we're there in the first place.

I recently visited a mourner in Jerusalem. I sat silently, patiently. After several minutes, he looked up and said, "I remember the tragic way your father died. How long has it been?" I replied but, internally, I was a little taken aback. Why was he bringing up my father at *his* Shiva house? It took me a moment to realize that, for some reason, he didn't want to talk about his parent's death right then. Maybe he just wanted to remember that bad things also happen to others. I don't know why, but at that moment, he needed to talk about my tragedy, not his. For many reasons, I didn't want to revisit that tragedy, but the mitzvah of Shiva was to comfort him, and this is how he wanted to be comforted.

The message is clear: Don't try to discover what words of comfort the mourner needs until you hear what the mourner needs from you. And be prepared to sit in uncomfortable silence. Perhaps, at that moment, that's precisely what he needs.

Many people urged me to write a chapter about the right things to say at a Shiva house. To do that, I would need to understand the needs of every mourner - past, present and future! It's an impossible task. Every person grieves differently. Each will experience the same five stages of grief, but never identically. We all navigate mourning at our own pace. We all interpret each stage in our own way.

Let me illustrate. Rabbi Lamm describes inadvisable ways to comfort a mourner.[59] One is to say that G-d needed our loved one more than we did. Now, flash back to Atlanta, Georgia in the early 1990's. We are attending a graveside funeral officiated by Rabbi Emanuel Feldman. A beloved child has succumbed to a tragic illness. As we listen to Rabbi Feldman, the boy's grief-stricken mother cries, "G-d wanted him more than I did." The Rabbi pauses, nods solemnly and repeats the mother's words. Was Rabbi Lamm wrong? Is this how to console mothers who have lost a child? Of course not, but this specific mother found consolation in the idea that G-d had taken her son with love. With great compassion, Rabbi Feldman demonstrated that this notion can only be expressed by the mourner, not by someone trying to comfort her.

So are we supposed to just sit there and say nothing during our Shiva call? After all, Job's friends sat with him for a whole week and never said a word! Is that the idea? I have a friend who thinks so. He will walk into a Shiva house and remain silent until, just before leaving, he says Judaism's traditional words of comfort. I was always impressed with his ability to remain quiet until my brother, z'l, passed away. The other visitors didn't notice his silence, but I did. Even when I addressed him, he just nodded and said nothing. I don't know why, but it bothered me. I don't know what I wanted to hear from him, but I wanted to hear something. In other words, Job's friends did the right thing for Job, but if they had been paying me a Shiva call on that particular day, it would not have been the right thing for me. I can't say this often enough: What happens in a Shiva house isn't up to the visitors. It is up to the mourner. And his comforters must help him on his terms. Of course, it's not easy! But that is what our Rabbis require of us: to fulfill the mourner's needs, just as Job's friends did.

What if the mourner says nothing? When I was in high school, a student lost his father, and our class paid a Shiva call. He lived out of town, so a large group of us traveled by bus to see him. We sat next to him and, for literally ten minutes, not one word was spoken. It was very awkward, and no one knew what to do. Finally, our teacher asked about his father's life, and our classmate started to speak. Our teacher knew that in that particular situation, further silence would have embarrassed the boy. That also takes wisdom: when *not* to be quiet. That is why paying a Shiva visit is so difficult.

When it comes to comforting a mourner, there are so many clichés. It is better to avoid them altogether than to try to figure out if they might be appropriate. Here are just a few clichés: "This will make you a stronger person." "They're in a better place." "You'll get over it." "Time heals all wounds." Although well-meaning, these expressions suggest that the mourner will forget his loved one. But the mourner doesn't want to forget his loved one. Whatever he will feel later is irrelevant.[60]

In an article about Shiva etiquette, Dr. Bernie Kastner, a psychotherapist living in Israel, asserts that even though he lost a 19-year-old son to illness, he would never say to a bereaved parent, "I know what you're going through." Those words seem so natural, so appropriate, but every mourner and situation is unique. One person's pain is never identical to another's.[61]

So what should we do if choosing the right words seems beyond our reach? The best thing is to pay a Shiva call when conversation is not expected: during prayer services. It is an important Mitzvah for men to ensure that there is a minyan, or quorum of ten men, for all prayer services. Sometimes, not knowing if there will be a minyan distresses mourners deeply. Conversely, knowing that, no matter what, there will be a minyan relieves them tremendously. This gives you the opportunity to show you care without relying on words.

Although it doesn't replace a Shiva visit, sending a condolence card can benefit both you and the mourner. Your handwritten note can convey thoughts and feelings you might find difficult to express in person, especially in front of other visitors. What's more, a note lasts beyond Shiva and can comfort a mourner later in the grieving process - and beyond.

Another thing to remember is that multiple visits are allowed! If you can visit a Shiva home more than once, especially a home with fewer well-wishers, you will bestow great honor to both the mourners and the loved one they have lost.

I will never forget my recent conversation with a non-observant Jew. He considered the sensitivity of Judaism's Shiva laws and customs nothing short of brilliant. Remaining silent until the mourner speaks reflects this sensitivity. It highlights our Rabbis' commitment to mourners. But more than that, it teaches their visitors an essential lesson: We are here to hear.

6

A Quick Guide

*T*he following table offers mourners a quick guide to review when they experience the loss of a loved one. It should not replace consultation with a Rabbi. Rather, we hope it will help mourners without immediate access to Rabbinic support. Unless otherwise indicated, the laws in this list apply to both men and women.

This guide was originally prepared in Hebrew by Rav Yosef Zvi Rimon, Rav of the Southern section of Alon Shvut and director of

Merkaz Halachah V'Hora'ah, located in Israel's Yeshivat Har Etzion. We thank him for permitting us to translate and include it here.

We are deeply grateful to Rav Hillel David of Brooklyn, New York, for reviewing the table and making important additions and suggestions.

Although this book deals with the Shiva experience, this chart reviews laws and customs preceding and following the Shiva process.

~ BEFORE BURIAL ~

SUBJECT	The Law	Sources & Notes
Who is an Onein?	A person whose deceased father, mother, brother, sister, son, daughter or spouse has not yet been buried.	
Brachot (Blessings) and Mitzvot	An Onein may not perform positive mitzvot, nor may he recite blessings or prayers. However, he may not violate any negative commandments (prohibitions).	Shulchan Aruch, YD 341, Yad Ephraim: You wash your hands in the morning and for bread, but without a Bracha (Blessing). You should count Sefirat Ha'omer without a Bracha (Pitchei Teshuva 341, Paragraph 6) and you put on Tzitzit without a Bracha. (Minchat Shlomo Vol. 1, 91, 25:3) TEFILLIN - There are varied opinions about putting on Tefillin after the burial if it is on a different day than the death. The general custom is not to put on Tefillin the day of the burial at all, but a Rabbi should be consulted when the funeral is delayed at least one day.

SUBJECT	The Law	Sources & Notes
When the burial takes place the next day...	He should recite Ha'mapil and Kri'at Shema al Ha'mita before retiring.	Minchat Shlomo, Part 1, 25:9 If someone dies on Friday and it is impossible to bury him before Shabbat, relatives are not considered an Onein until Shabbat ends.
What is forbidden to an Onein?	Bathing, s'machot (any activity that increases one's happiness), exchanging greetings, getting a haircut, studying Torah, praying, eating meat and wine, marital relations, and conducting non-essential business. (If he is in partnership with a non-mourner, a Rabbi should determine how business should be conducted.)	Shulchan Aruch and Rama 341:5 If he has a specific physical problem that requires bathing, he may shower, preferably in lukewarm water and one limb at a time.

SUBJECT	The Law	Sources & Notes
What is permitted to an Onein?	He may leave his house to recite Tehillim (Psalms) as a protection for the deceased. He may sit on a regular chair (some sit on or close to the floor at mealtimes).	Shulchan Aruch and Rama, ibid. Sitting- Gesher Hachaim- Vol.1, 18
Does an Onein recite Kaddish for the deceased?	Ashkenazim do not, but Sephardim do say Kaddish (word for word with the Chazzan) if they go to synagogue.	Taz, YD, 376:4 (The Mishna Brura states in OC 71:7 that Ashkenazim can say it under certain conditions.) Sephardim – Yalkut Yosef 3:17. On Shabbat, most say you can say Kaddish (Taz, 306:4), but the Zohar says not to say Kaddish until after the burial.

BEFORE BURIAL

SUBJECT	The Law	Sources & Notes
What does an Onein do on Shabbat?	He must fulfill all commandments and make all Brachot and is allowed to eat meat and drink wine. Marital relations are forbidden. He should only recite Havdallah a day after the burial, but without a candle or spices.	Shulchan Aruch, YD, 341:1-2 (Yad Ephraim)
May he change clothes before the funeral?	He is allowed to change clothes in order to tear a different garment than the one he is wearing.	Gilyon Maharsha, Yoreh Deah 340
When does he say the Bracha of Dayan Ha'emet and when does he perform K'riyah (make a tear in his clothing as a sign of bereavement)?	Although the law is to fulfill both obligations upon hearing the bad news, today's custom is to perform them at the funeral.	Shach, Yoreh Deah, 340:3 Gesher Hachaim Vol. 1, 4:6

A Quick Guide

SUBJECT	The Law	Sources & Notes
How does he perform K'riyah?	He tears his garment while standing.	K'riya while standing - Shulchan Aruch and Rama Yoreh Deah 340:1 – if he tore while sitting, he must tear again, but he doesn't have to repeat the Bracha of Dayan HaEmet (it is not connected to the tearing). For his parents, he should tear by hand, but for other relatives, he can tear with a tool (Shulchan Aruch, YD, 340:14). The custom of tearing for a parent is for someone else to start the tear with a tool and he continues by hand.
How much does he tear?	A Tefach: 8 centimeters (3.1 inches). For a parent, he tears on the left side. For other relatives, on the right side.	Tearing a Tefach- Shulchan Aruch, Yoreh Deah, 340:3 (Taz 340:6 and Schach 340:19) For all relatives, he only tears his outer garment but for a parent, he tears all his clothes except an undershirt, Tzitzit, sweater, or coat. (SA, YD 340:9, 10) The custom is for a woman to only tear the upper garment and for reasons of modesty, to use safety pins to close the tear.

BEFORE BURIAL

SUBJECT	The Law	Sources & Notes
Does he recite the Bracha of Dayan Ha'emet on Shabbat?	He recites the Bracha but does not perform K'riya. If he did tear his garment, he does not have to tear again after Shabbat.	Chachmat Adam 151:18 and Shulchan Aruch Yoreh Deah 340:28

~AFTER BURIAL~

SUBJECT	The Law	Sources & Notes
Placing a Stone	After the burial, it is customary to place a stone on the grave.	Gesher Hachaim Vol. 1, 16:7. Placing flowers is a custom of non-Jews, and they wither and die. A stone represents eternity because, like our soul, it never dies.
Shoes	The mourner removes his leather shoes immediately after the burial.	Shulchan Aruch, 375:1
The Row of Comforters	Those in attendance move at least 4 Amot (app. 6.5-7.5 feet) from the grave and form one or two rows. The mourner walks in front of or between the rows as the people recite words of comfort.	Talmud Sanhedrin 19a, Gesher Hachaim Vol. 1, 16:7. Those present console the mourner by saying "Hamakom Yenachem Etchem B'toch Sha'ar Avelei Tzion Vee'rushalayim", which means "May G-d comfort you amongst the mourners of Zion and Jerusalem". The Sephardic custom is to say "Min Hashamaim Tenuchamu" which means " May you be comforted from the Heavens." (These are also the parting phrases used upon leaving a house of mourning)

SUBJECT	The Law	Sources & Notes
Washing the Hands	All attendees wash their hands after the burial. The mourner takes the washing cup himself, not directly from another's hand.	Shulchan Aruch, YD 376:4, Rabbi Akiva Eiger The custom in Jerusalem is not to dry your hands in order to leave the impression of the funeral on them. This custom has spread to other places (Beit Lechem Yehuda, ibid.). One is not allowed to enter a building without washing his hands.
The beginning of Shiva	Even if the funeral ends up to 17 minutes after sunset, Shiva has already started if the mourner sits down outside the cemetery to receive comfort or performs another act of mourning. (e.g., removing leather shoes, etc.)	Gesher Hachaim, Vol. 1, 19:4 Some only allow this up to 13.5 minutes after sunset. (If this can be done, the mourner has already completed one day of Shiva.)
Seudat Havra'ah – The meal of comfort, served after the funeral	The meal should be from the food of others, and not his own. On Friday afternoons, close to Shabbat, the custom is not to feed the mourners the Seudat Havra'ah.	Shulchan Aruch, YD 378:1,5 The custom is to feed the mourner round rolls and hard boiled eggs (Pnei Baruch 7:10) In general, he can be counted as part of a group of three who say Birkat Hamazon together but most say he is not allowed to participate in this after the Seudat Havra'ah (Shulchan Aruch, YD 379:5, Schach)

A Quick Guide

~ SHIVA ~

SUBJECT	The Law	Sources & Notes
Difference between first three days and the rest of Shiva	It once was customary not to visit the mourner during the first three days of Shiva, but today, this practice is rarely followed.	The only practical difference seems to be in the exchange of greetings (see below). During the first three days, the mourner cannot ask how someone is and if someone asks him, he cannot answer but he should let them know he is in mourning. After that, he still cannot ask, but can answer if someone asks him. (Shulchan Aruch YD, 385:1)
Wearing Shoes	Forbidden throughout Shiva. However, the mourner still recites the Bracha "that you provide me with all my needs," usually omitted when wearing shoes is forbidden.	Mishna Brura, 554:31 However, the Vilna Gaon says not to make this Bracha on Tisha B'Av or Yom Kippur
Bathing	The mourner may not wash his entire body. However, he may wash parts of his body in lukewarm or cold water. It is permissible to bathe when he is dirty.	In honor of Shabbat, he can wash his whole body in lukewarm water, one limb at a time. Most say a sensitive person can wash regularly during Shiva but a Rabbi should be consulted.

SUBJECT	The Law	Sources & Notes
Makeup and Cream Application	It is forbidden to apply makeup. One can apply cream for dry skin. One may use fragrance-free deodorant.	Shulchan Aruch, YD 381:6
Torah Study	Only studying the laws of mourning or other sad topics is permitted. Some authorities permit the recitation of Psalms.	Talmud Yerushalmi, Moed Katan, 3:5 – "since the Torah makes us happy…."
Customs in a house of mourning	All mirrors are covered and a candle is lit throughout the week of Shiva.	Pnei Baruch 10:4 You don't have to cover the mirrors in rooms that are not used and some cover pictures of people as well. On Friday afternoon, the mirror covers are removed (Shmirat Shabbat K'hilchata, Vol. 2, 65:8)
Meat and Wine	It is permissible to eat meat and drink wine.	Shulchan Aruch YD 378:8
Sitting/ Sleeping	It is customary to sit on a low chair, not higher than three Tefachim (approximately 9.5 inches) from the ground. The custom today is to sleep in a standard bed.	Some say the chair should be no higher than one Tefach (app. 3.5 inches) and this is accepted by some Sephardim. Someone weak or a pregnant woman can sit on a normal chair. (Aruch Hashulchan, YD 387:3, Gesher Hachaim Vol. 1, 20:11)

A Quick Guide

SUBJECT	The Law	Sources & Notes
Marital Relations	Marital relations are forbidden (even on Shabbat), but physical contact is permissible.	It is best to be stringent and not to engage in kissing and hugging, and to separate the beds. (Shulchan Aruch, YD 383:1)
Exchanging Greetings	We do not greet a mourner and he does not greet anyone throughout the week of Shiva. Shaking hands with a mourner is permissible (Har Tzvi, YD: 290)	Shulchan Aruch YD 385:1- The mourner can nod to a visitor in place of a greeting. Some say the use of the word "Shalom" (which is one of G-d's names) is forbidden, but saying "Good Morning" or "Good Evening" is permitted, and others argue (Beer Haitaiv, YD 385:2; Kol Bo on Aveilus, Part 2, 4:7; Gesher Hachaim Vol.1, 21:7:5)
How to begin to console the mourner/ the way to console a mourner	It is better for the mourner to initiate dialogue and, at times, silence is the most appropriate way to console. However, a visitor may speak first if the silence causes the mourner embarrassment. When consoling, visitors must remember that the unique needs of each mourner are paramount.	Moed Katan 28b, Shulchan Aruch 376:1 (see chapter 5 for further details) (Maimonides Hilchot Avail, 13:1) Upon leaving the house, the visitor says the same phrase that is said at the funeral when the mourner walked through the rows. (see above)

SUBJECT	The Law	Sources & Notes
Laundry/ Laundered Clothing	Doing laundry and wearing laundered clothing is forbidden.	It is permissible to change from a garment that is dirty or full of perspiration (Gesher Hachaim Vol.1, 21:10). Ashkenazim extend the basic prohibition through the Shloshim period.
Haircut/ Shaving	Forbidden until after Shloshim, and afterwards, it is only permissible if someone tells the mourner that he looks bad, needs to shave, etc.	Shulchan Aruch, YD 390:1
Nail Cutting	It is forbidden to cut nails throughout Shloshim, unless it is done in an atypical manner (e.g., biting or tearing them).	Shulchan Aruch YD, 390:7 - to tear them off in an abnormal manner is also allowed during Shiva
Doing Work	Work is forbidden, except for necessary household tasks. Time-sensitive work, especially when refraining from it may cause great financial loss, is permitted under certain conditions.	Shulchan Aruch and Rama, YD, 393:1; 380:22

SUBJECT	The Law	Sources & Notes
Leaving the House	The mourner should not leave his house, but if there is a great need, there is room for leniency, especially after the first three days of Shiva.	Shulchan Aruch and Rama, YD, 393:1,2; Gesher Hachaim, Vol.1, 21:13 – if one has to leave, it is better to do so unobtrusively (e.g. at night).
Preparing for Shabbat	The mourner may start preparing for Shabbat approximately 1.25 Halachic hours (Sha'ot Zemaniyot) before sunset.	Gesher Hachaim, Vol.1, 21, 12:3- Some say that if it is necessary, he can begin up to 2.5 Halachic hours before sunset
Mourning on Shabbat	The mourner does not mourn publicly on Shabbat. He may wear Shabbat shoes and clothing. He may not study Torah, except to review the weekly Torah portion, if this is his normal practice.	Gesher Hachaim Vol.1, 21:12 He should not receive an Aliyah to the Torah on Shabbat, but if they call him up, he can take it. (Shulchan Aruch, YD, 400:1) There are varied opinions about singing Shalom Aleichem but our custom is that the mourner says it (Shmirat Shabbat K'Hilchata, Vol.2, 65:15)

SUBJECT	The Law	Sources & Notes
Saturday night – Motzei Shabbat	He says "Baruch Hamavdil bein kodesh l'chol," removes his leather shoes and davens Maariv. Some authorities say he is obligated to change clothes immediately, but others say he can be lenient for an hour or two without having to tear his Shabbat clothing.	Rama, OC 553:2; Gesher Hachaim, Vol.1, 20:3:9,10
Kiddush Levana	If there is time for it after Shiva, he should wait. If not, he should only say the Bracha.	Mishna Brura, 426:11
Ending Shiva	The mourner sits briefly after Shacharit. The comforters tell him, "Get up," and the Shiva is completed.	Shulchan Aruch and Rama, YD, 395:1
Cemetery	In Israel, it is customary to visit the deceased's grave on the last day of Shiva.	Shulchan Aruch 344:20 - this is mentioned in terms of visiting righteous people, but the custom has developed to visit all graves.

SUBJECT	The Law	Sources & Notes
Changing your synagogue seat	Ashkenazim change their synagogue seat for the year of mourning, whereas Sephardim only do so for 30 days.	You have to move 4 Amot (6.5-7.5 feet). On Shabbat, you only move for 30 days. (Gesher Hachaim, Vol. 1, 22:3)
Smachot- Happy Occasions	The mourner does not attend any festive event for 30 days, except if he is mourning the loss of his parents, in which case this restriction lasts for twelve lunar months.	There are specific cases where this is permitted- please consult your Rabbi

~ PRAYER SERVICES IN A HOUSE OF MOURNING ~

SUBJECT	The Law	Sources & Notes
The Amidah- Shemoneh Esrai and all Brachot (Blessings)	These are recited.	
Section of Sacrifices- Korbanot (Morning Service)	We recite the portion of the Tamid Offering, the Mishnayot of Aizehu Mikoman, and the paragraph of Rabbi Yishmael but we skip the portions of the other sacrifices and the formulation of the incense (Pitum Haktoret).	Shulchan Aruch AC 554:4- This entire section is said but the Rama in AC 559:4 says not to say Pitum Haktoret. Sephardim say the entire section (Yalkut Yosef- Vol.7, 10:6)
Tachanun (Morning and Afternoon Services)	This is not recited.	Mishna Brurah, Shulchan Aruch, AC, 131:20 – We do not want to activate the attribute of judgment in a house of mourning
Avinu Malkeinu during the Ten Days of Repentance or on a fast day (Morning and Afternoon Services)	This is recited.	Eliyahu Rabba, 131

64   A Quick Guide

SUBJECT	The Law	Sources & Notes
Keil Erech Appayim (Monday and Thursday Morning Service before reading Torah)	This is not recited.	Gesher Hachaim, Vol. 1:20,3,4
Lamnatze'ach (Morning Service)	This is not recited.	Gesher Hachaim ibid. – In order that the attribute of judgment will not be activated through the mention of "troubled days".
Uva L'Tzion Go'el (Morning Service)	This is recited, but the sentence beginning with "Va'ani Zot Briti" is skipped.	Gesher Hachaim ibid. – There should not be a covenant established while in mourning. Also, the Torah is called "covenant" and a mourner is prohibited from learning Torah during Shiva.
Reading the Torah (Monday and Thursday Morning Services only)	We read the Torah, but the mourner is not allowed to be called up for an Aliyah, even if he is the only Kohein present.	Shulchan Aruch, YD 384:2 – A mourner is allowed to take out and return the Torah to the Ark, and to lift or tie it up (Taz Par. 1)

PRAYER SERVICES IN A HOUSE OF MOURNING

SUBJECT	The Law	Sources & Notes
Yehi Ratzon after Torah Reading	The custom is not to recite it, but logic dictates that it should be recited, unless Tachanun is not recited in synagogue on that day.	Daat Kedoshim, Chazon L'Moed, 16:6 (Rav Grossberg) – This is not like Tachanun, but rather is a request that we are making to G-d, which does not preclude its being said in a mourner's house. However, since the custom is not to say it, we do not. (If there is no specific custom that is known, it can be said.)
Additional Reading of Psalm 49 (Weekday Morning and Evening Service, according to Ashkenazim)	It is added at the end of the service. If there is no Tachanun said that day in synagogue, Psalm 16 is added instead.	Gesher Hachaim Vol.1,20,3,4
V'hi Noam (Saturday night evening service)	This is recited.	Gesher Hachaim Vol.1: 20,3,9- Some say the first sentence should be omitted but most are accustomed to say it in its entirety.
Havdala – Saturday night	If the mourner himself says it, he should skip the introductory paragraph and start with the Bracha over the wine.	Gesher Hachaim Vol.1: 20,3,10 – He should also say the Bracha on the spices.

SUBJECT	The Law	Sources & Notes
Hallel on Rosh Chodesh	Ashkenazim do not recite it since it includes expressions of happiness, but the Musaf Rosh Chodesh service is said (Mishna Brura, 131:4). Some visitors follow the custom to go into another room, recite Hallel and then complete services with the mourner. (If the deceased died in the house, Hallel is omitted entirely.) Sephardim all recite Hallel, except for the mourner (Yalkut Yosef Vol.7: 10,13)	The Mishna Brura says that the visitors do not say Hallel after they leave the mourner's house, while others say they should say it later (Shulchan Aruch Harav, OC, 131) If Rosh Chodesh falls out on Shabbat, the Mishna Brura says the mourner should say Hallel.
Hallel on Chanukah	Ashkenazim do not recite it, but the visitors must either recite it in another room or recite it later in their homes. Sephardim, including the mourner, recite it (Yalkut Yosef, ibid.).	Hallel on Chanukah is an integral part of the day, and therefore, must be said at some point by the visitors (it is said by the mourner according to the Sephardim)

PRAYER SERVICES IN A HOUSE OF MOURNING

SUBJECT	The Law	Sources & Notes
Birkat Kohanim – The Priestly Blessing – Morning Service (only applies to parts of Israel)	Ashkenazim outside of Jerusalem do not say it. Kohanim leave the room before R'tzei (Biur Halacha, Shulchan Aruch, OC, 128:43). Sephardim and Ashkenazim in Jerusalem say it, except for - if he is a Kohein - the mourner himself (Yalkut Yosef-Vol.7, 10:6).	Gesher Hachaim-Vol.1:20,3,5 If the blessing is not said, some say the entire paragraph should be omitted by the Chazzan.
Selichot - Morning Service	The Selichot are abridged: "Zchor Rachamecha" until "Shema Koleinu" is omitted; "Shema Koleinu" is said and the rest is omitted.	Gesher Hachaim Vol.1 – 20,3,4
Prayers on Shabbat – if a minyan is conducted in the mourner's house	A complete prayer service is conducted, so as not to mourn publicly on Shabbat.	Gesher Hachaim Vol.1:20,3,9 The mourner is not given an Aliyah. If he is the only Kohein, he can receive an Aliyah (Rama, Shulchan Aruch YD 400)

Afterword – Shiva Is Over. Now What?

The day a mourner gets up from sitting Shiva can be very trying. Shiva gave him the opportunity to talk about his loved one, to be surrounded by friends and family who shared his anguish. Now he is alone, facing grief all by himself. True, there are customs of mourning that will continue throughout the Shloshim period or, following the loss of a parent, throughout an entire year. But as difficult as Shiva might have been, forcing the mourner to face his loved one's death, the absence of its supportive atmosphere is even harder. Now the mourner must return to "normal" after the devastation he has experienced.

Shiva is named for its seven-day duration because those seven days are important. In essence, they enable the mourner to embark on a journey, a journey whose duration is uncertain, but whose destination will eventually be reached.

How does a mourner, shaken and disorientated by his loved one's death, take the next steps on his journey? It depends. No two mourners are alike, be it during or after Shiva. So although the following insight might not help everyone right after Shiva, its message is too powerful to withhold.

In *Consolation*, Rabbi Lamm shares an analogy he heard from Rabbi Joseph B. Soloveitchik. When tragedy makes life seem incoherent and meaningless, when that tragedy compels us to doubt the existence of a benevolent Creator, we need to envision two sides of a beautiful tapestry:

"Imagine you are looking at the back of a magnificent unlined tapestry hanging in a museum. You see a profusion of threads strung wildly in every direction, a riot of colors with no apparent purposeful arrangement; no fine embroidery, only stitching – an appalling mess. But then you realize that you are looking at only the underside of a brilliant work of art and, after staring at it, the picture begins to fall into place......You know that if you could see its front side you would find it breathtakingly beautiful."[62]

Our perspective of G-d's world is only from the back of the

tapestry – we see the mess of strings that initially seem to have no pattern to them. If we had G-d's view, we would see that every single thing and every single event in His world works together to create a beautiful picture. We would realize that everything, bad or good, that happens to us has a purpose and a part in this wonderful piece of art called life.

Taking this message to heart might be difficult, but it can help us on the road to overcoming our grief. Painful questions may plague us along the way. Remembering that G-d has a plan is one way to find comforting, lasting answers.

We hope that anyone who has to sit Shiva will have the blessing of maximizing its purpose: to begin to cope with the death of a loved one. We pray that we all will be granted the opportunity to view the front of life's tapestry very soon. We pray that the day will soon come when we will know no more sorrow.

HaMakom Yenacheim Et'chem B'toch Sh'ar Avelei
Tzion V'Yerushalayim.
May you be comforted among the mourners of Zion and Jerusalem.

Appendix - KADDISH

KADDISH IS RECITED ONLY IN THE PRESENCE OF A *MINYAN*.
MOURNER:

YISGADAL v'yiskadash
sh'mayh rabo.　　　　　　　　　　יִתְגַּדַּל וְיִתְקַדַּשׁ שְׁמֵהּ רַבָּא.

May His great Name grow exalted and sanctified

CONGREGATION RESPONDS: Omayn — אָמֵן

B'ol'mo di v'ro chir-usayh.　　　　בְּעָלְמָא דִּי בְרָא כִרְעוּתֵהּ.

in the world that He created as He willed.

V'yamlich malchusayh,　　　　　וְיַמְלִיךְ מַלְכוּתֵהּ,

May He give reign to His kingship

b'cha-yaychōn uvyōmaychōn　　　בְּחַיֵּיכוֹן וּבְיוֹמֵיכוֹן

in your lifetimes and in your days

uvcha-yay d'chol bays yisro-ayl,　　וּבְחַיֵּי דְכָל בֵּית יִשְׂרָאֵל,

and in the lifetimes of the entire Family of Israel,

ba-agolo u-vizman koriv.　　　　בַּעֲגָלָא וּבִזְמַן קָרִיב.

swiftly and soon.

V'imru: Omayn.　　　　　　　　וְאִמְרוּ: אָמֵן.

Now respond: Amen.

CONGREGATION RESPONDS:

Omayn. Y'hay sh'mayh rabo m'vorach　　אָמֵן. יְהֵא שְׁמֵהּ רַבָּא מְבָרַךְ
l'olam ul-ol'may ol'ma-yo.　　　　לְעָלַם וּלְעָלְמֵי עָלְמַיָּא.

Amen. May His great Name be blessed forever and ever;

MOURNER CONTINUES:

Y'hay sh'mayh rabo m'vorach　　　יְהֵא שְׁמֵהּ רַבָּא מְבָרַךְ
l'olam ul-ol'may ol'ma-yo,　　　　לְעָלַם וּלְעָלְמֵי עָלְמַיָּא,

May His great Name be blessed forever and ever;

yisborach v'yishtabach v'yispo-ar　　יִתְבָּרַךְ וְיִשְׁתַּבַּח וְיִתְפָּאַר

blessed, praised, glorified,

v'yisrōmam v'yisnasay　　　　　וְיִתְרוֹמַם וְיִתְנַשֵּׂא

exalted, extolled,

v'yis-hador v'yis-ale v'yis-halol　　וְיִתְהַדָּר וְיִתְעַלֶּה וְיִתְהַלָּל

mighty, upraised, and lauded

sh'mayh d'kudsho b'rich hu　　　שְׁמֵהּ דְּקֻדְשָׁא בְּרִיךְ הוּא

be the Name of the Holy One, Blessed is He,

CONGREGATION RESPONDS:

B'rich hu.　　　　*Blessed is He.*　　　　בְּרִיךְ הוּא.

Appendix - KADDISH

°l'aylo min kol °לְעֵלָּא מִן כָּל
beyond any

FROM ROSH HASHANAH TO YOM KIPPUR SUBSTITUTE:
°l'aylo l'aylo mikol °לְעֵלָּא לְעֵלָּא מִכָּל
exceedingly beyond any

birchoso v'shiroso בִּרְכָתָא וְשִׁירָתָא
blessing and song,
tushb'choso v'nechemoso, תֻּשְׁבְּחָתָא וְנֶחֱמָתָא,
praise and consolation
da-amiron b'ol'mo. דַּאֲמִירָן בְּעָלְמָא.
that are uttered in the world.
V'imru: Omayn. וְאִמְרוּ: אָמֵן.
Now respond: Amen.

CONGREGATION RESPONDS: Omayn — אָמֵן
Y'hay sh'lomo rabo min sh'mayo יְהֵא שְׁלָמָא רַבָּא מִן שְׁמַיָּא,
May there be abundant peace from Heaven,

v'cha-yim olaynu וְחַיִּים עָלֵינוּ
v'al kol yisro-ayl. וְעַל כָּל יִשְׂרָאֵל.
and life, upon us and upon all Israel.
V'imru: Omayn. וְאִמְרוּ: אָמֵן.
Now respond: Amen.

CONGREGATION RESPONDS: Omayn — אָמֵן

MOURNER BOWS, THEN TAKES THREE STEPS BACK, BOWS LEFT AND SAYS:
Ō-se sholōm bimrōmov עֹשֶׂה שָׁלוֹם בִּמְרוֹמָיו,
He Who makes peace in His heights,

MOURNER BOWS RIGHT AND SAYS:
hu ya-a-se sholōm olaynu הוּא יַעֲשֶׂה שָׁלוֹם עָלֵינוּ,
may He make peace upon us,

MOURNER BOWS FORWARD AND SAYS:
v'al kol yisro-ayl. V'imru: Omayn. וְעַל כָּל יִשְׂרָאֵל. וְאִמְרוּ: אָמֵן.
and upon all Israel. Now respond: Amen.

CONGREGATION RESPONDS: Omayn — אָמֵן

MOURNER REMAINS IN PLACE FOR A FEW MOMENTS, THEN TAKES THREE STEPS FORWARD.

Reproduced from the ArtScroll Siddur, with permission of the copyright holders, ArtScroll / Mesorah Publications, Ltd.

Endnotes

1. *Habayit Hayehudi,* Part 1, Aharon Zakai p. 226

2. *The Mourning Handbook,* Helen Fitzgerald, Simon and Schuster, 1994, p. 30

3. *On Grief and Grieving,* Elisabeth Kübler-Ross and David Kessler, Scribner Publishing, 2005 pp. 7-24

4. *When There Are No Words,* Charlie Walton, Pathfinder Publishing, 1996 p. 24

5. *Consolation,* Rabbi Maurice Lamm, p. 21

6. *Consolation,* p.53

7. *Honoring and Mourning Adoptive and Step Parents,* Le'ela, June 2001, no.51 and *Mourning Abusive Parents,* Hakirah, the Flatbush Journal of Jewish Law and Thought, Winter, 2010, Volume 9

8. *Yoreh Deah* 476:3

9. *How to Go On Living When Someone You Love Dies,* Therese Rando, Ph.D., Lexington Books, 1988 p.17

10. Hakirah, page 197

11. *Pirkei D'Rabi Eliezer* Chapter 17 (Choreiv Edition) uses this as the source for the seven days of Shiva.

12. *Genesis* 50:10

13. The Ibn Ezra (Genesis 50:8) disagrees with this and says the seven days occurred after the burial and the Torah is not in chronological order.

14. See Chapter 4 – the custom is to no longer say this blessing

15. *Mishneh Torah,* Hilchot Aveil, 1:1

16. Technically, someone may start sitting Shiva before the burial. Sometimes, for example, the deceased is buried in Israel while some mourners remain in the United States. In that case, the departure of the deceased is considered closure, and Shiva commences for those staying behind.

17. *Genesis* 37:35

18. *Consolation,* pp 200-201

19. Most notable is Maimonides who says that if you have the chance to either comfort a mourner or visit the sick, the Shiva visit takes precedence because you are helping out both the living and the dead. (See Note 31)

20 *Daas Chochmo U'Mussar,* Vol.3, 295. The concept of Nosei B'ol… is presented in Ethics of Our Fathers, 6:6. There is a wonderful description of this concept and its relationship to mourning in The Neshama Should Have An Aliyah, Rabbi Tzvi Hebel, Judaica Press pp.27-30

21 *Chochmo U'Mussar,* Vol. 1, 1

22 *Echoes of the Maggid,* Mesorah Publications, pp 68-70

23 *Gesher Hachaim,* Volume 2, Chapter 27

24 See Chapter 6

25 See Chapter 6

26 *Parshat Vayechi* 219

27 *The Neshama Should Have An Aliyah,* Hebel, page 28

28 *Numbers* 25:11

29 *Shu"t Minchat David,* Vol. 2, Chapter 73

30 *Igros Moshe,* Orach Chaim, Volume 4, Chapter 40:11

31 *Mishneh Torah,* Hilchot Avail, 14:7

32 *Light and Consolation,* Shmuel Glick, Schocken Institute, page 190

33 *Responsa of Rashba* Vol.1:828

34 See Chapter 2 and the discussion about following the lenient position in mourning practices.

35 *Shulchan Aruch,* YD, 387:2

36 *Torat Ha'adam,* page 150

37 *Kol Bo on Aveilus* (Chapter 4:1:14)

38 *Talmud Moed Katan* 27b

39 *Pnei Baruch,* Chapter 7:1

40 *Shulchan Aruch,* YD, 378, 9 (Rama)-the Vilna Gaon adds that the eggs should be peeled for the mourner.

41 *Shulchan Aruch* YD 375:1 (Ramban)

42 *Tur Shuchan Aruch* YD 382:1

43 *Kol Bo on Aveilus,* Chapter 4:1,11; Beer Heitev, Shulchan Aruch OC, 90

44 *Consolation,* pp 94-95

45 *Consolation,* p 97

46 *Consolation,* p.20

47 *Talmud Bavli, Masechet Moed Katan,* 15b

48 *Talmud Bavli, Masechet Moed Katan,* 15a, *Mai'Olam V'ad Olam,* Gavriel Goldman, Magid Publishers p.164

49 *Shulchan Aruch,* YD, 390:1

50 *Leviticus,* 10:6

51 *Talmud Bavli, Masechet Moed Katan,* 14b

52 *Mai'Olam V'ad Olam,* p. 153

53 *Shu"t Har Tzvi,* Yoreh Deah, Siman 290 – There was a custom in England for the consoler to bless the mourner with long life and shake his hand. Rabbi Tzvi Pesach Frank permitted this because it was not an actual greeting.

54 *Psalms* 116:15

55 *Mai'olam V'ad Olam,* p 269

56 *Machzor Vitri,* Chapter 144

57 For our benefit, the story describes the soul's suffering in physical terms but, of course, we can't grasp what that suffering really is.

58 *Living a Year of Kaddish,* Ari L. Goldman, Schocken Books, 2003, p.185

59 *Consolation,* pp 305-311

60 *Good Grief, Bad Grief,* page 51

61 *What to Say At A Shivah Call,* Dr. Bernie Kastner, 5/12/11 Five Towns Jewish Times

62 *Consolation,* pp.155-156

Personal Reflections

About the Author

*Y*igal Segal received a Masters Degree in Administrative Science from Johns Hopkins University and was ordained by the Ner Israel Rabbinical College in Baltimore, Maryland. After serving for five years as the Director of Development of the Torah Day School of Atlanta, Georgia, he launched the Jewish Literacy Foundation in 1998. Yigal lives with his wife and children in Jerusalem. He encourages feedback, questions, and comments via email at guidetoshiva@gmail.com

The Jewish Literacy Foundation

*T*he mission of the Jewish Literacy Foundation is to promote Jewish literacy through the creation and distribution of quality materials to Jewish adults either directly or through existing Jewish organizations.

More Than A Tear is one of the many innovative, educational projects made possible by the Jewish Literacy Foundation

Jewish Literacy Foundation

600 Reisterstown Road, Suite 514 • Pikesville, MD 2120
212-444-1918 • www.jliteracy.org • jliteracy12@gmail.com

OTHER TITLES AVAILABLE ARE:
Rosh Hashanah Yom Kippur Survival Kit
Chanukah: Eight Nights of Light, Eight Gifts for the Soul
Death of Cupid
One Hour Purim Primer
Survival Kit Family Haggadah